The Case of the Six-Sided Dream

Poems by

Matthew M. Monte

BLUE LIGHT PRESS ✦ 1ST WORLD PUBLISHING

1st WORLD
PUBLISHING

SAN FRANCISCO ✦ FAIRFIELD ✦ DELHI

Winner of the 2017 Blue Light Poetry Prize

The Case of the Six-Sided Dream

Copyright ©2018 by Matthew M. Monte

1ST WORLD LIBRARY
PO Box 2211
Fairfield, IA 52556
www.1stworldpublishing.com

BLUE LIGHT PRESS
www.bluelightpress.com
bluelightpress@aol.com

BOOK & COVER ART & DESIGN
Melanie Gendron
melaniegendron999@gmail.com

FRONT COVER DESIGN & AUTHOR PHOTO
Matthew M. Monte

FIRST EDITION

ISBN 978-1-4218-3815-1

Acknowledgements

I am grateful to the editors of the following journals and anthologies who have published some of these poems.

Side Stream, Issue 25: To Luthiers and Their Makers
Poets 11 Anthology, 2016: Perfect Lunch #2
Poets 11 Anthology, 2016: If Green Street Could Walk
Poets 11 Anthology, 2016: History Lesson
Snackbar Collective, Issue 3: Like San Francisco

"A Partial Bestiary for Burning Libraries" is inspired by the reportage of veteran war correspondent, Joshua Hammer, who wrote, "The Bad-Ass Librarians of Timbuktu: And Their Race to Save the World's Most Precious Manuscripts."

"To Be a Citizen is to Be a *Poeta*" is inspired by Alejandro Murguía, who said in his acceptance speech as Poet Laureate of San Francisco: "…I would propose that we adopt as the most honorable address for a fellow citizen of San Francisco, the City of Poets of the Americas — not doctor, or esquire, not even mayor or supervisor — but the most honorific and respectful way to address a fellow human being — *Poeta*!"

for Steph and Miles

Contents

The Case of the Six-Sided Dream 9

A Partial Bestiary for Burning Libraries 10

To Luthiers and Their Makers 13

Polaroid Mom 14

Everywhere I Go 16

I Read Virgil 18

In Bed, the Body 19

Like San Francisco 20

Post-Postmodern 21

To Be a Citizen is to Be a *Poeta* 23

The Mist is Settling on Everything 24

Which Way, Flower Girl? 25

Hitchhiking in Waiatarua 26

In Which the Grammarian Gives Bad Advice 27

Perfect Lunch #2 29

Valencia Street 31

Poplar: The Improbable Invention of Pointillism 32

Wall Clock 33

If Green Street Could Walk 34

Walking the Neighborhood 36

My Grandfather Sings Verdi 37

Geese Pass the Open Skylight 38

Un-Free Verse Is So Antiquated 39

Hardly a Still Life 40

History Lesson 42

About the Author 45

The Case of the Six-Sided Dream

Downstairs they're cooking rice
to go with something that used to run off leash
and trilling along with the TV.

Through the far wall, our landlord is dying in his sleep,
a little each night.

In the front yard he tore the last tree from the block.

Out back he wills his drought upon the blackened hedge.

Our southern neighbors are hammering nails again.
There's more metal than wood in their walls
and a picture hung
for every day since Creation.   In an unaccountable

caesura of neighborly silence

rain sweeps the roof
riprapping a Roland Kirk rag, like
when the drummer comes brushing in,
and you know the reeds are right behind,
calling all dimensions to a collision
in tune.

A Partial Bestiary for Burning Libraries

I think of burning libraries,
Alexandria for one.

I think of the Taliban looking to burn every scroll
in Bamako that might reveal Islam's
thirst for inquiry.
I think of the real radicals, librarians
secreting truths downriver:

Constellations of gazelle skin and papyrus.
Ink etched on chary genealogies
older than the astronomer's proofs, but not what he's proven,
and generations of scholarship
visiting and revisiting his transit of Venus in the margins;
a distance of suns running nocturnal rapids
out of Timbuktu.

I think of the librarian who lives
over his corner store. He sighs in smoke over Carthage, still,
and Jaffna more recently,
bemoaning bachelorhood and a dusty degree in Classics
before extinguishing the neon and ascending to his desk
to tap-tap away the overdue hours.

He remembers aloud, lips moving in Oxford-accented Tamil,
until I approach the counter.

> "There is a name for every known species
> glossed in the slippage of a dead language
> for a living science," he says.

There is talk of a palm leaf library back in Sri Lanka,
chloroplasts imprinted with the Buddha's words,
harvesters of light,
sutras burning in protest of impermanence,
if I have my politics correct.

Some nights I hear his typewriter keys clacking
from down on the sidewalk
while out for my insomniac stroll.
I look into his eyes and down at the cold silver in my palm,
do the math on jungle fires.

"Do you think there is a poem for every species?
One unaware of the other, mostly,
a dying ratio of dying concern?" he asks.

Now I know he's seen me out walking.
It brings to mind larger questions
of balance.

Our neighborhood was teetering
on the brink of extinction
until the liquor store opened its doors.

"Water to wine is just a parlor trick," he says,
"but it always draws a crowd
so here I am."

"You must know," he adds, surveying his magazine rack,
"words are all we have
for assembling granite from ash."

Sitting before the rows and rows
of bottles, redolent with his Tiparillos,
he doesn't touch a drop.

This is his potshot at martyrdom, his
counting out change
while drawerfuls, reams of
Olivetti-sparked words, ignite his upstairs apartment:
a library of the mind burning down present tense San Francisco,
burning in disbelief, he believes
for nobody else.

To Luthiers and Their Makers

Voices carry in treeflesh and gutstring you
wordless virtuosi of time.

Play to critical earnings, knowing age splits,
cadence drops

the concentric signatures.

Scale their heights, gather elements. The luthier
as well

builds his guitar ironically;

for sound will find its coda, the raked
earth die, the brave planet

wither, a tested seed.

Yet trees held you for 1,000 years
before fingers coaxed

their marrow's honey
that makes a rising song.

Polaroid Mom

Her face is a faint voice dipped in darkness.
Calling before I see her, though we are instant
intimates in one another's presence.

We are impatient with our slow image
coming through the reverse burn,
crepe of ash, disintegrating into color.

Now she comes along with everything behind her:

Blue sky in a kind-of-blue ocean,
emptied of blue man-O-war
piled upon the tideline

with very, very white people obliterating
winter from their bodies.

What has become of our species?

We hold the image, developing its answer
a ringless hand on each border.
My childhood camera weighing around her neck,
lilac in a smiling stranger's hair —
a shock unloosed flicks my neck, a brief third rail thrill
brings our picture to life.
The little girl tugs at her mom's rolled-up jeans
dying to see what we're made of:

I kneel beside her driftwood teepee,
blonde head poking through the door.
This is the image she wanted
so Mom reluctantly pointed and shot

blushing, too, like this face from the neighborhood
coming into focus.

Lines deliquesce into a crispness
surprising us three.

Before it's too late, I smile and wave
and wander up the dunes
as if I could back into the Polaroid dark
beneath all this aching light.

Everywhere I Go

Everywhere I go they leave me flowers
but never a note.

Is it a pageant or a funeral I've won?
They offer no clues but strewn petals
and sunken gardens
wreathed in statuary.

Just today they a left rose garden along my commute.
Though clearly dear to someone, I still work a day job.
It's a mixed message if you ask me, this incessant adoration.
Royalty kept roses but they bloody the hands.

On the way home, I saw their grandest gesture yet:
a crystal palace crowded with flora craning for light
in the high cupolas of humid glass.
Attendants beckoned from the translucent portals.
"Yes, you," they nodded as I slowed to a stop.
Nobody answered my questions,
not even the docent when we paused,
dizzy with oxygen,
mute in the Amazonian wing,
mooning over the bromeliads.

I read that some celebrities
spend six figures a year sending flowers
to friends and heads of state
for everything from "Salutations," to
"Sorry about your civil war."

But all the famous people I know are dead.

I like when the bouquets arrive.
Last week they delivered a swaying clutch
of date palms. You should see the view —
and how much fruit! —
when you shimmy up the trunks.

And though it quickly outgrew the vase,
I love the redwood grove that arrived
by unmarked general delivery.

Leis from a place called Palolo arrive once a month.
I wind them around my landlord's neck
with all the dead presidents I can spare.

He's always been allergic to rent control,
and the plumerias don't help.
    I think I like this secret admiration.

I Read Virgil

After a sleepless night, I read Virgil,
cradling first light in my hands.

Pages resound. Ancient words rise —
freedom exists beyond Troy's broken walls.

I stand beside my bookshelf at the window
looking at the morning streets.

I raise my hand to the garbage man
making his Thursday rounds, a man who has it all.

He nods and goes on his way,
loaded down with future archeology.

Weather rages. Power lines rattle the air.

      Jealous gods hurl their elements
at us mortals and the moaning jaws of the garbage truck.

Every line held, it seemed, so that

voices once without a book
ferried in biremes might
cross time's doldrums
and find another city
in these ever-dying hands.

In Bed, the Body...

In bed,
the body is a long resting thing.

Even with light spilling through the slats
it seems a great distance to somebody else's toes,

mysterious as a map of rumpled country
with no known language.

Strange to marvel at the lack of elevated thought,
everything exposed, the rest in bedclothes.

White walls in their early illumination
offer up a silent empty house

and erase the question

of what mind
and whose body.

So reach and grip those feet
and greet the fact of this body:
bones and sinew in delicious revolt,
before settling, once again, into the pillow and the glorious doze
that feather-floats
between states.

Like San Francisco

Like San Francisco, that great imitator
of Old World masters, and *maestra*
of *perspectivo*, I linger on the possibilities
inherent in hills.

Even with the throb of a twisted ankle
I hobble across your incandescence
where so many soldiering veterans of misfortune
sleep mangled at the train stops.

I litter the ground with spare change,
silvery bread crumbs leading to meager
food, drink, shelter, hope.

Some streets you can see for undulating miles.

What marvel is next?
What heartbreak
         is next?

Junkies on a rotting sofa down Alice B. Toklas Street
push rust and opium into their tattered arms.
         Alice B., she's just an alley, see, but
we try to reclaim
how she spent her best days
at the address where it really ends —
         In Paris with Gertrude and the sitting room full of Picasso
shattering perspective across great tiled plains
one for each particle of both cities' lights.

Post-Postmodern

Goya had a black phase.
Picasso held his blues.

Lorca leant us a green phase
that lasted one poem long:
"Green, I want you green," he began.
But Spain murdered the only seed,
buried beneath the leaden soil of an unmarked garden — and yet,
to read is to reel one's age
back into Time's sunken corolla,
where Nature defers to Art's color but once,
leaves its blackened coda.

To be postmodern is to be
ever present in the worst possible way:
overflowing art of commentary;
obsessively referencing my-my-my favorite subject
to the point of numbness. We've become
themes in search of a body.

Which is why
I need to view more Catholic art.

Why do museums full of aching flesh
always put me in place?

Who can say why I feel affinity
when hammered to mythology's pith?

Or that I never rise
though utterly oriented,
by the spiked iron and the coarse wood,

tethered to earth by plainspoken carpentry
so that I might meditate
upon a faith in *Guernica*.

Born in a post-Age
I step back into Modern
culminating in death
whether you believed the bombs or not.

Do we all seek the death of an age?

No postscripts but for letters.
No footnotes but for scholars.

Though we might allow a manifesto
ripe with rejection
for future elders to herald the turning
that ate everything from innocence
again.

To Be a Citizen is to Be a *Poeta*

To be a citizen is to be a *poeta*.
Once, mere citizenship
verified my Molotov rage.

But I'm rethinking this citizenship thing,
because glass against the wall and a river of flame
oxbowed from its source wears only
the heavy, unyielding yoke.

       I turn to what?

Bills, deliberate in their length?
Forces to be filibustered in footnote font,
freighted with other fates and a clean conscience —
a sociopathic epic paid in free verse?

       Instead, we might return to

Concision.
     Precision.

Great minds turning the language.

Finding form
     A simple page
          Facts of freedom
               Born on ink

The Mist is Settling on Everything

The mist is settling on everything.
The train splashes past. The house rumbles in its wake.
The heat clicks on in the middle of spring.
I close all the windows.

Way across San Francisco the sun is blazing.
Everyone is sure of it.
Out here by the ocean the land simply draws more water.
The sky is weighted, low slung, not bothering to fall, what
with water rising to meet it.

Out here, our street is like the others:
Alphabetical, neatly numbered in a nautical grid,
now submerged beside the park
where the oldest trees sway like rooted water lilies
buoyed in the sky.

Ornithologists consult swell maps and crane their necks
up to canopies where
birds flit like water bugs
skating the even stratospheres.
        It is a rare migratory season, a day in length if that.

Already, the sun is settling on everything. Waters recede.
I open a second story window, just above the flood zone again,
drainpipes done with their music.
Seated upon the neighbor's olive branch
a crow thinks to caw
waiting for the ground to reappear
glistening black in remnants of thinning silent mist.

Which Way, Flower Girl?

in the evening
she pulls dripping stems
from black buckets

bouquets
                        put away for the night
        with thorn-pricked hands

                she
                    comes to the door
                    once more
                      leaning in the jamb
sucking the blood of her thumb
and turns the sign
to closed

— OR —

in the evening
she pulls dripping stems
from black buckets

bouquets
                        put away for the night
        with thorn-pricked hands

                she
                    comes to the door
                    once more
                    leaning in the jamb
i suck the blood of her thumb
and turn the sign
to closed

Hitchhiking in Waiatarua

my roadside image
    mirrored in
        last night's rain
           silt settled
              puddle-cupped and clean
                    cloud forest
                      mist falling
                          no wind

                         only

                         no wind
                      mist falling
                    cloud forest
              puddle-cupped and clean
           silt settled
        last night's rain
    mirrored in
my roadside image

In Which the Grammarian Gives Bad Advice

Whatever you do
Learn to use the tools
Do not set out on Monday
To make miracles from sentences
First learn to read and
How to hold a pen
Not much comes of craft
No matter what they say around the workshop
Planing their wooden voices
Curls of music left only for the sweepers

Learn the trade
Words for money
Spinozahood may come later
Or not at all
Even though you know how to weigh a colon
Like an anchor
Keep the list from drifting
Semi-colons like breaths
Periods
For
Finality

Em dashes
En dashes
You know best
Ellipses and parentheticals
For trailing and packaged thought

And asides

There will be many questions
And fury
Measured in the reader's
Deep understanding
Of your words

Perfect Lunch #2

I lean into Vallejo Street
and tell the tourists up top
while I munch nasturtium flowers,

"It's named after Cesar, the poet
not the Spanish general
in your Lonely Planet death march."

But I can see I've lost all credibility
right here on the summer stairs
chewing my cud like a lazy-ass brahma.

Zig and zag
and we are at Golden Boy
for pizza squares and a Coke.
Across the way, inquiring about
a lap steel guitar in the window, I am
handed a bruised beauty that
wails like 200 years' worth.

"I cannot pay our way, not yet, my sweet."

Espresso around the corner in a brown demitasse with
matching saucer and the jukebox
blaring *bel canto* to the curb.
I drink and leave
my empties atop the newspaper dispenser.

Zig and zag
and fall into the Bookstore
the last frontier, where
in the stacks

Martin Buber waits on me.
I and Thou are about to take our leave when

an agile clerk piles
new-pressed David Meltzer hardcovers
next to the register.

Warm in my hands,
two sages later,
I am half a days' wages down Broadway
where the paying gig's
watch-full hour
waits.

Valencia Street

I never understood apparitions
until you disputed my form;

until a cat purred into the void of my chest, until
I absorbed the dark room, diluted the high ceilings; until
silent flicker and fractal of the TV erased me
and dreamsleep
lost its taste for me.

In the morning I left through the keyhole,
latches and bolts straining against
Valencia Street and the rain
we needed so badly.

I used to believe poets inhabited your block
perched on fire escapes, pens in hand,
eyes ash-smeared with insomnia of waiting, but
had they existed
surely they would've invented me, turning the corner
beneath February
and a tease
of early blossoms.

Discarding these notions, I gathered my Self, and took up
where I'd left off,
filling my body with illumination,
swallowing one word at a time,

     remembering:

I am borrowed demarcation
aurora of the latest expression.

Poplar: The Improbable Invention of Pointillism

Slender to its swaying heights
Against a palette horizon
Wind's hand at minute brushwork
Of gold leaf fading hours

Ink last
A silhouette
Casting dusk to its borders
A winking canvas emerges

Day puts down its colors
Resting with Seurat
To ponder the dying season

Collecting summer's last
And gravity in their eyes
They pulled the heavens together
And found a cast of lights
Each in their solitude
Calling for union

Wall Clock

our wall clock metronome
our wood and metal corazón
eternal adagio
movement accents every upswing
pendulous brass
swaying in a silence

between

time's borrowed shape
that heliocentric koan we range

If Green Street Could Walk

If Green Street could walk
with you, lunch in hand, if it could
move from brick building
hillside shadow
cross to the pier,
she would lean over the railing at your
memory colored water, verdigris, which

because she is so
so fluent in green
knows it to mean *verde* and *gris*
green and grey
virgin and ancient and

you, too, are so
so fluent in green like the close
shades of chromaticism unfurling from

a tin whistle *maestra*
echoing her scales up and down
your view

of Treasure Island —
all water buried brick
grown over tides
and temblors.

Lunch settles down a shared gravel gullet,
swallows workaday pride.

Back on land
the trollies go up and down up

and down the sun bright promenade.
Blinding patina miracle of green
streets cross the tracks to lay me down, Green Street, she
addresses the paying day once more,
proffers her salty kiss
and waits at the door.

Walking the Neighborhood

Walking the neighborhood
    I hoped to see you
    down the block of shops. I hoped

to see you in a window
gesture at a menu, or
weigh a pair of pomegranates, maybe
gather with friends
outside the bookstore to
lean beneath the trees.

But there are no trees for leaning.
Cement is still wet on the stumps.
We have no bookstore,
gatherers gone in the risen rent.
Pomegranates are forever out of season.
Nobody orders off the menu and

windows stare darkly where
    down the block of shops
    I hoped to see you.

My Grandfather Sings Verdi

In the dream,
my grandfather sings Verdi.
I never knew my grandfather
except from the photos.
In the dream,
my grandfather sings Verdi
at a town hall meeting,
when San Anselmo is small
and he is the mortician
and the mayor,
singing to his present constituents
and future customers.
In the dream,
he sings a cheerful aria
that defies basic physics
the way major keys dealing in dark themes do.
I listen
beside the local accordionist, who accompanies him,
flexing the air through that strange invention.
It is a crowded hall
but I can see my father's father is
really singing at me.
I don't speak a word of Italian but
that doesn't seem to matter
they way it never does
to the dream.

Geese Pass the Open Skylight

Their music announces them

to where I stand breathing
October air
wreathed in sighs
clouding the kitchen chill.

Alone, I believe
I hear them alone. Deluded or not
the best ear believes it listens purely

to the rise of honks and winged air
passing my roof. Any second

       I expect a dawn thick with feathered bodies in formation
flying south, so full is their coming.

Only the sky
and its dying chorus,
fading with the fog,
return a tunneling square of light
to these silent, empty rooms.

Un-Free Verse is So Antiquated

"Un-free verse is so antiquated," tweets

A tulip-mouthed pilgrim into her phone.
Once, she escaped rain beneath a bandstand
When Minsk was purged of men, save those of stone.
Flush with books, in poverty's whimsied hand,

She recited Homer to draining skies
Ringed by men undone from hourglass tide.
Recast skin, free of apparatchik ties,
I, the quarried dead, revived in word, vied

For tulip-mouthed kisses, grateful for breath.
She fled my form, lips sugared with lotus,
Shedding truths, like so many a shibboleth,
Until her gift for reading gave notice.

Now she rides the train, a straight shot to town.
Force of character tweets her discontent:
"Lashed to the day, my darkling sirens have flown."
(All but one alit beside her lament.)

She says, "Poetical wax doesn't pay,
I'm down to over-the-shoulder readers."
Standing this close, what could I possibly say?
Once I bore the stone of party leaders?

I came to place my hands upon your ears
And melt the scars of common resignation,
To walk you from this country dulled by years
And relight the music of creation.

Hardly a Still Life

Van Gogh's sunflowers are
vibrating as we speak, Vincent and his
mad mix of oil,
hardly a still life.

Sun comes up.
Sun goes down.

This is to say I've seen a thing or two.
I've collected so many images on the way.
Lest we refuse,
garbage is a didactic poem,
carefully placed as a burger wrapper.
What is your contribution to archeology?

That is to note
what careless curators we've become.
Every night the images roll slowly, slowly,
rising to fullness that cannot sleep,

pushing waves upstream, every image in concert,
sufficient to reverse a river's course: consider this
force for a moment.

Sometimes there are surprises.

Like when the tide slackens and the sand parts
where the waters meet. Heaved
upon the shallows, a glistening shoal of beach glass,
a prism for each incidence of light.

Not quite fossils
but a ground down cultural ambition.
What do we want?
Vessels for beverages. This is our legacy.
No Grecian urns for a future Keats,
just booze and soda and maybe milk.

It is a careless curator's second chance
to reconsider the matter
of greatest importance:
            attention
and where to place it.
Image is not the thing.
Now is the thing.

Bask in trembling light
made by so much glass,
lit from a nearby star.
Know what you mean
as you make your way.

History Lesson (for Lawrence Ferlinghetti)

Unlived history is
a seed of doubt, deferred
when you meet the players
in our graves and tomes,

     or when you sit up in the middle of the night.

"I have lived so many years…"
A strange utterance, given your age.
It falls from conversation where
someone exhales a scrim of smoke —
or were they candles? —
spent in a party
you exit from sleep to your
dim house
scattered with nightlights
for visiting family who don't know their way as you
tiptoe amongst sleeping relations.

     A laptop screen is winking in the kitchen.

     Good thing you own a telescope.
Things get lost on the Internet, that strange
universe — hardly a vessel of consciousness —
it's saddest illusion:
that multitudes contain you.
So glide through the sleeping house,
part the curtains in the snoring living room.

     The in-laws say, secretly,
     they've always doubted your buying power.
But the stars are out.

Out the window,
out there, you flew in from elsewhere on that stretch of sky, once.
It's easy to believe in past lives when considering the present.

A niece smiles in her sleep.
Pills on the coffee table
keep the elder hearts regular,
though stars are fading
like this bout with wakefulness.

Passing the uncorrupted
sleep of innocence,
experience pulls blankets up to chins,
adjusts stuffed animals.

Passing laden bookcases it seems
you have hauled entire aisles from
Mr. Ferlinghetti's reading room
up to this word-crammed flat
one volume at a time
and to the brink of divorce — but some day
they'll all thank you.

For these containers
of consciousness are
old newfound words, the next ones
on the path, assembling and sorting;
solid meanings locking against
one another, earning their keep, a foothold
in stories that tell you stories you tell
towards your ascension to what
you could not say, except that

life has you
history has found *you*,
not the other way around.

How un-"American" yet
how at ease, are these
sleepwalking bones

in San Francisco
a republic all its own.

About the Author

Matthew M. Monte grew up near San Francisco, California and went to the University of Hawaii-Manoa, where he studied botany. His fiction, poetry, book reviews, and essays have appeared in *Sidestream, Creosote Journal, Transfer, Ashcan Magazine, The Snackbar Collective,* and the *Poets 11 Anthologies* (2014 and 2016). He lives in San Francisco with his wife and son.

His debut collection, *The Case of the Six-Sided Dream,* won the 2017 Blue Light Poetry Prize.

To schedule readings, book signings, or say hello:

Website: matthew-monte.com

CPSIA information can be obtained
at www.ICGtesting.com
Printed in the USA
LVHW04s0844241018
594370LV00026B/168/P